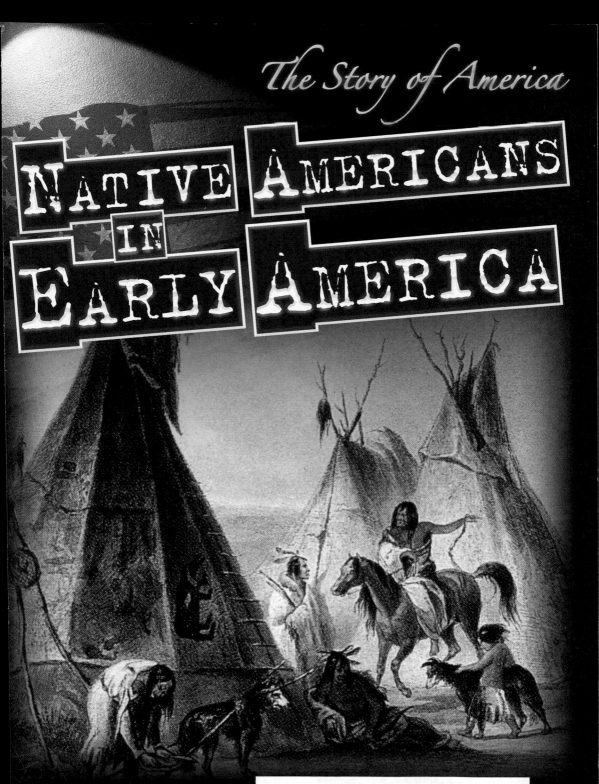

The Story of America

NATIVE AMERICANS IN EARLY AMERICA

By Mark Harasymiw

Please visit our Web site, www.garethstevens.com. For a free color catalog of all our high-quality books, call toll free 1-800-542-2595 or fax 1-877-542-2596.

Library of Congress Cataloging-in-Publication Data

Harasymiw, Mark.
 Native Americans in early America / Mark and Therese Harasymiw.
    p. cm. — (The story of America)
 Includes bibliographical references and index.
 ISBN 978-1-4339-4773-5 (pbk.)
 ISBN 978-1-4339-4774-2 (6-pack)
 ISBN 978-1-4339-4772-8 (library binding)
 1. Indians of North America—History—Juvenile literature. I. Harasymiw, Therese. II. Title.
 E77.4.H36 2011
 970.004'97—dc22

                                          2010039137

First Edition

Published in 2011 by
Gareth Stevens Publishing
111 East 14th Street, Suite 349
New York, NY 10003

Designer: Daniel Hosek
Editor: Therese Shea

Photo credits: Cover, pp. 1, 8, 11, 26 MPI/Getty Images; pp. 4–5 James Randklev/The Image Bank/Getty Images; p. 6 Marilyn Angel Wynn/Nativestock.com/Getty Images; pp. 7, 18, 23 Hulton Archive/Getty Images; p. 12 David David Gallery/Getty Images; p. 13 Ted Spiegel/National Geographic/Getty Images; pp. 14–15 SuperStock/Getty Images; pp. 17, 29 Buyenlarge/Getty Images; p. 19 Robert Giroux/Getty Images; pp. 20–21, 25 Stock Montage/Getty Images; p. 22 Kean Collection/Getty Images; p. 24 Library of Congress, Prints & Photographs Division.

Printed in the United States of America

CPSIA compliance information: Batch #CW11GS: For further information contact Gareth Stevens, New York, New York at 1-800-542-2595.

Contents

Words in the glossary appear in **bold** type the first time they are used in the text.

First Peoples

The story of America goes back further than the 1492 arrival of Christopher Columbus. People came to North America as early as 20,000 years ago, perhaps even earlier. They crossed a land bridge that connected northwestern North America and northeastern Asia at that time. Some chose to stay north—in the Arctic and subarctic regions—while others ventured south. Although hunters and gatherers at first, many relied on agriculture by about 1000 B.C.

These people—known as Paleo-Indians—were the ancestors of the Native Americans present when Europeans first came to America. They settled in distinct environments all over the land that would become the United States. Each unique native culture was rich with understanding of nature and complex in tradition and religion.

These Paleo-Indian rock carvings, called petroglyphs, are found in Canyonlands National Park in Utah.

Ice Age Land Bridge

Although the Bering Strait now separates Asia and North America, a land bridge between the two appeared as a result of the **Ice Age**. During this period of colder global temperatures, glaciers grew by absorbing massive amounts of seawater. As a result, sea levels dropped, exposing previously covered land. At its widest, the expanse across the Bering Strait stretched about 1,000 miles (1,600 km) from north to south. The land bridge may have lasted as long as 18,000 years.

DID YOU KNOW?

Native Americans in Peru built pyramids about 500 years before the Egyptians built them in Egypt!

The Northeast Tribes

The Northeast region of North America included today's Canadian coast south to North Carolina and west to the Ohio River valley. Two types of houses reflected the forested environment of this region. Wickiups (or wigwams) and longhouses were wood-framed structures covered with plants or bark. The native inhabitants had access to rivers, lakes, and the Atlantic coastline. Dugouts—boats carved from logs—and birch-bark canoes provided transportation.

Animals such as deer, moose, turkey, and fish were abundant sources of food and clothing. Maize (corn), beans, and squash were the main crops. They were also the three main spirits of the Iroquois tribes' religion. Other Northeast tribes included the Algonquin, Huron, Wampanoag, Mohican, Pequot, Ojibwa, Mohegan, Ho-chunk (Winnebago), Fox, and Illinois. Many used the Iroquoian and Algonquian languages.

wickiup

longhouse

DID YOU KNOW?

The word *wickiup* means "dwelling" in the Fox language.

Leading the Tribe

In Northeast tribes, the leader was often called a *sachem*. Each sachem ruled an area called a sachemdom. The position of sachem was passed down from father to son, or to a daughter if no son was available. Sachems conducted business with other tribes, acted as judges, and assigned hunting grounds. They had assistants who were sometimes chosen by the tribe's senior women.

This image shows Indian leaders from several different tribes across America. An Iroquois tribesman is shown at left.

The Southeast Tribes

The Southeast Indians lived from what is now North Carolina south to the Gulf of Mexico and west to the Mississippi River. With a warm climate and long growing season, farming was a major part of life. A huge plateau between the Appalachian Mountains

This picture shows several fishing strategies of Seminole fishermen. The fence at left keeps fish in a limited area so they're easier to spear.

and the Atlantic coast was the most fertile region and therefore the most populated. Hunting for large game such as bear took place in the fall to provide meat and clothing in colder weather. Fish and wild plants were plentiful year-round for coastal tribes. Some Southeast Indians used **blowguns** for hunting.

Among the most famous Southeast tribes were the Cherokee, Choctaw, Chickasaw, Creek, Seminole, Natchez, Caddo, and Apalachee. Besides wickiups, there were earthen dwellings as well. Later, chickees—houses on **stilts** with thatched roofs and no walls— were ideal in the swampy, hot land of Florida's Seminoles.

The Five Civilized Tribes

The Cherokee, Choctaw, Chickasaw, Creek, and Seminole were called the Five Civilized Tribes by white settlers. In the early 1800s, these tribes feared being forced to move from their lands by American settlers. They decided to adopt some American culture, such as language, farming methods, and even slavery. **Assimilation** didn't work. In 1830, the Indian Removal Act took their land. Some had to be forcibly removed. About 4,000 Cherokee people died following what came to be called the Trail of Tears.

DID YOU KNOW?

A favorite game of the Natchez and other tribes was called chunkey. People threw poles at a rolling disc for points.

The Plains Tribes

From Canada south to Texas and from the Rocky Mountains east to the Mississippi River, the North American plains didn't seem welcoming. Dry and windy with few trees, the region was home to Plains Indians for one reason: bison. The massive animals—once numbering 60 million—provided meat, fur, fuel, and bones. Hunting expeditions sometimes lasted weeks, but could feed and clothe a family for a year. Grassy plains and river valleys to the east were centers of Plains agriculture. Indians created earth-lodge villages there. Later, tepees made of bison skin became the transportable homes of the hunters.

Plains Indians included the Mandan, Hidatsa, Omaha, Pawnee, Arikara, and Crow. In the 1700s, Spanish explorers brought horses to North America. The horses made hunting easier, and previously agricultural people—such as the Sioux, Blackfoot, Cheyenne, Comanche, and Arapaho—became hunters, too.

Horses Help the Hunt

Plains Indians once dressed as wolves to get close to bison. Then they used bows and arrows to kill the animals. Yet another method was to drive a herd over a cliff's edge. The arrival of horses in the 1500s changed bison hunting. On horseback, Indians could surround herds and easily shoot them. However, horses also caused conflicts. The more horses a tribe had, the more bison they could get. Tribes began taking other tribes' horses, and rivalries became common.

This painting from 1887 suggests the excitement, speed, and danger of a bison hunt on the American plains.

DID YOU KNOW?

Plains people invented a sign language as a way for tribes speaking different languages to communicate.

The Southwest Tribes

Native Americans of the Southwest inhabited **mesas**, canyons, deserts, and mountains. This area includes modern-day southern Utah and Colorado, Arizona, New Mexico, and a large part of Mexico. Little rain, hot climate, and rocky terrain seem an unlikely combination for a successful culture. Most

The stacked homes of the Zuni are shown in this painting from 1895.

early communities survived by gathering seeds, roots, and cactus fruits. They lived in caves. Later, the Colorado River and Rio Grande created opportunities for growing crops, such as corn, beans, squash, and cotton. Birds, snakes, deer, and jackrabbits were other sources of food.

Southwest Indians included the Pueblo (such as the Zuni and Hopi), Navajo, Apache, Yumans, Pima, and Tohono. The Pueblo people built apartment-like homes of adobe and stone. The Pima, settled near the Gila River, built houses of adobe mud, cactus, and willow.

DID YOU KNOW?

Maize, or corn, was first grown in what is today Mexico over 6,000 years ago. It was unknown in Europe until explorers returned with it.

Sand Painting

Sand painting wasn't just art to the Navajo and Pueblo Indians. It held healing power. Sand, charcoal, and other colorful materials were arranged on smooth sand. The sick person sat on the painting and was covered by sand from it. When the **ritual** was completed, the painting was destroyed. For years, the Indians wouldn't allow sand paintings to be copied or photographed. An error was made on purpose so each design would keep its power.

The Great Basin Tribes

The Great Basin in western North America is named for its bowl-like landscape, surrounded by the Rocky Mountains and the Sierra Nevada. This area includes today's states of Utah and Nevada as well as parts of Oregon, Idaho, Wyoming, Colorado, Arizona, Montana, and California. A large amount of the region's water—notably the Great Salt Lake—is salty, and much of the land is desert. Thus, agriculture was difficult, and most tribes were hunters and

On a journey west across the continent, explorer Meriwether Lewis was warmly greeted by the Shoshone Indians in 1805.

gatherers. Seeds, roots, pine nuts, and small game such as rabbit and snake were the Great Basin diet. Northern and eastern people adopted horses and bison hunting after the Spanish arrived.

The Great Basin was home to the Washoe, Mono, Paiute, Bannock, Shoshone, Ute, and Gosiute. As hunters and gatherers, family groups moved when necessary.

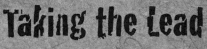

Taking the Lead

Native Americans of the Great Basin didn't have permanent leaders. A leader was only followed as long as he was successful in finding food and in war against other tribes. If people lost faith in a leader, they would join another leader's band or create a new one. Bands had few members and were constantly on the move. They organized this way so they didn't exhaust the food supply in an area.

DID YOU KNOW?

The people of the Great Basin ate almost anything that moved—except coyotes, because they were revered in legends.

The California Tribes

The tribes of today's California and Baja California (Mexico) enjoyed a varied environment. The Pacific coast, the Sierra Nevada, plateaus, basins, deserts, and wetlands offered plentiful food. Major tribes, some with languages named for them, included the Hupa, Yurok, Pomo, Yuki, Wintun, Maidu, Chumash, and Yana.

Many California Indians lived in groups of a few hundred to a few thousand people. Most lived in permanent villages. Gathering was the easiest source of food; acorns were very important. Fishing and hunting provided whatever else was needed. Farming occurred only along the Colorado River. Housing varied from round, wood-framed, single-family dwellings to multifamily, apartment-like buildings. Dugouts and reed rafts were used for fishing and transportation. The Chumash people of Southern California made excellent boats of planks and **asphalt** that could carry up to 20 people.

This photo from around 1924 shows a Pomo woman cooking in front of her home.

The Last of the Tribe

In 1908, California surveyors found four Native Americans living in the wild. They were Yahi, related to the Yana people. In 1911, one of the four appeared near Oroville, California. He was starving and frightened. His friends called him *Ishi*, which means "man" in Yana. Ishi was given a home at a University of California museum. Thought to be the last Yahi, he taught others about his people's traditions until he died in 1916.

DID YOU KNOW?

California's native languages have been described as more varied than those found in all of Europe.

The Northwest Tribes

The Native Americans of the Northwest occupied the Pacific coast from what is now northern California to Alaska. This is a region of mountains and **temperate** rainforests. Fish, birds, sea mammals, and wild plants were abundant, so agriculture wasn't necessary. Villages were built near water, and large, rectangular homes had removable walls and roofs. Villages were organized into groups called "houses" with ranks such as chiefs, nobles, commoners, and slaves. Northwest tribes include the Tlingit, Haida,

Fishing tribes built platforms over rivers from which they would spear or net fish, a practice that extended into modern times.

Tsimshian, Kwakiutl, Bella Coola, Nuu-chah-nulth (Nootka), Coast Salish, and Chinook.

Celebrations called potlatches were important to the Northwest cultures. The host of each potlatch showed wealth by giving gifts to guests. A potlatch could elevate the rank of the host. Sometimes, rival families in competition tried to outdo each other with potlatches.

The Totem Pole

Although the Northwest Indians are well known for them, totem poles weren't a traditional part of their culture. Totem poles became common when Indians began trading fur to Europeans for iron tools. The poles weren't religious objects. They were created to display the **crests** of the owner or in remembrance of a loved one's life.

DID YOU KNOW?

Some Northwest Native Americans would let fish heads and fish eggs rot before eating them. They considered them high-quality foods.

◄ **totem pole**

The Plateau Tribes

Plateau Indians inhabited modern-day northern Idaho and Montana, eastern Oregon, eastern Washington, and southern British Columbia (Canada). The climate was similar to that of the Plains but milder. Mountains kept rain from hitting lower elevations. Grasslands and desert were the main setting for these hunters and gatherers, with permanent settlements found by rivers. Homes were multifamily and grass covered. Small, cone-shaped

An official from a railroad speaks with some Nez Percé Indians in 1853. The railroad would bring more settlers to the Plateau region.

houses were found at higher elevations. With the arrival of Spanish horses, Plateau people became bison hunters.

Among the Plateau Indians were the Salish, Flathead, Modoc, Nez Percé, Yakima, Kutenai, Spokan, Kalispel, Pend d'Oreille, Coeur d'Alene, Wallawalla, and Umatilla. Tribes sometimes formed partnerships. This was more likely in societies with a constant source of food, such as fish from the Columbia and Fraser Rivers.

Salmon

Salmon were an important source of food for both the Northwest and Plateau people. During the time when salmon were swimming up the river, white stones were placed below fishing platforms so the fishermen could see the fish more easily as they swam over the stones. Some villages also appointed a "Salmon Chief" to use magic to make the catch better.

DID YOU KNOW?

Plateau people often burned down a house if someone had died in it.

A New World Begins

The arrival of Christopher Columbus in 1492 was a turning point for Native Americans. The Spanish began establishing settlements in the Southeast in the late 1500s. The British, Dutch, French, and other Europeans followed in the seventeenth century.

Squanto—a Pawtuxet Indian—was an interpreter and guide for the settlers of an early colony at Plymouth.

In many instances, the initial relationship between Native Americans and Europeans was peaceful and friendly. At Jamestown, the first permanent British settlement in North America, the colony's first years were marked with hunger and sickness. The local Powhatan tribe provided meat and corn in exchange for European tools, clothes, and other goods. However, after a **drought** and British thievery, the Indians decided to stop trading food to the British. This resulted in a period of near starvation in Jamestown.

Farming 101

The Native Americans taught settlers how to plant crops together. Climbing plants, such as beans, were planted next to tall plants, such as cornstalks. Growing beans alongside corn was beneficial to corn. Corn (and most other crops) drain nitrogen—an element necessary for plant growth—from the soil. Beans, however, put nitrogen back into the soil. Another Native American farming method included burning the previous year's leftover crops. The ash made the soil more fertile for new plants.

DID YOU KNOW?

Pocahontas was the daughter of the chief of the Powhatan tribe.

◄ Pocahontas

As the number of colonists increased, a series of conflicts occurred in the Northeast. The Pequot War began in 1636 between the British and the Pequot Indians who lived along the Connecticut River. The British settlers had allies in the Narragansett and Mohegan tribes. Later, King Philip's War (1675–1676) ended with the destruction of many Wampanoag villages.

To the south, Spanish **conquistador** Hernando de Soto swept through the Southeast tribes in the mid-1500s. Beginning in Florida in 1539, he enslaved many as he headed north. The Natchez had little contact with Europeans until the late 1600s. However, a 1731 war with the French resulted in the near **eradication** of the tribe. Survivors were sold into slavery or adopted by other tribes.

Hernando ▶
de Soto

This engraving shows British colonists attacking a Pequot camp in 1637.

DID YOU KNOW?

In 1680, the Pueblo Indians of the Southwest revolted against their Spanish rulers and remained independent for 12 years.

Land Ownership

Native Americans and Europeans had different ideas concerning land. Europeans believed that each piece of land had an owner and that a country had a ruler who could make decisions for everyone. Native Americans didn't believe land had a permanent owner; people simply used it.

Diseases

The biggest killer of Native Americans during European settlement wasn't warfare but disease. After the Bering Land Bridge disappeared, the Native Americans weren't exposed to any other people or to European diseases. In addition, most Native Americans lived a healthy life in open spaces, compared to the lives of Europeans in crowded cities.

This 1805 painting of a Native American tribe portrays a ritual dance to heal the Indian on the stretcher in the left background.

The Europeans had lived with certain diseases for thousands of years and had developed some **immunity** to illnesses such as influenza, smallpox, measles, and cholera. Native Americans had no immunity, and the diseases spread quickly, even reaching farther inland than the Europeans had traveled. The weakest tribal members were the first to die. These included the elderly, who were the keepers of the tribes' oral histories and stories. This signaled the beginning of the end of many Native American cultures.

Zoonotic Diseases

Many of the diseases that were present in Europe originated in animals but passed on to humans. This class of diseases—called zoonotic diseases—included smallpox and measles. Many Europeans lived near their **domesticated** animals on small plots of land. Native Americans had almost no domesticated animals until the Europeans arrived, so they were free of zoonotic diseases. The number of Native Americans that died from European-carried diseases will never be known for sure.

DID YOU KNOW?

Perhaps 80 percent of all Native Americans died of disease within the first few decades of European arrival.

The Fight for the West

After the establishment of the United States, Congress gave lands between the Missouri River and the Rocky Mountains to the Native Americans. However, the migration of Americans to the West didn't stop. Many continued to trespass onto Native American settlements, which were centuries old or newly made after forcible removal from a previous homeland. Soon, Congress made it legal for Americans to take this land. No matter how much they fought, it seemed every Native American culture striving to preserve its way of life was at the mercy of the changing United States.

Timeline

AROUND 18,000 B.C.
Asian people begin to arrive in North America

1539
Hernando de Soto lands in Florida

1607
First permanent British settlement established

1492
Christopher Columbus arrives in the Caribbean

1565
First permanent Spanish settlement established

1636
The Pequot War begins

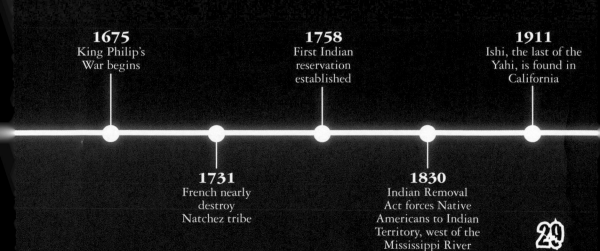

Taken around 1890, this photograph shows a Lakota Indian camp on the Pine Ridge Indian Reservation in South Dakota.

1675
King Philip's War begins

1758
First Indian reservation established

1911
Ishi, the last of the Yahi, is found in California

1731
French nearly destroy Natchez tribe

1830
Indian Removal Act forces Native Americans to Indian Territory, west of the Mississippi River

Glossary

asphalt: a brownish-black substance found in nature that hardens when it cools

assimilation: the process of one group taking on the culture of another group

blowgun: a long, narrow tube through which darts or pellets are shot by blowing

conquistador: a Spanish conqueror or adventurer

crest: a symbol of a family

domesticated: to make an animal used to living with or near people

drought: a long period of dry weather so that crops cannot grow

eradication: the act of destroying something completely

Ice Age: a period during which temperatures fall worldwide and large areas are covered with glaciers

immunity: a body's ability to resist disease

mesa: a flat, elevated area with steep sides that is smaller than a plateau

ritual: a formal ceremony

stilt: a supporting post that lifts a building above land or water

temperate: describing a climate with temperatures that are not very hot or very cold

For More Information

BOOKS

Brennan, Kristine. *Native Americans*. Philadelphia, PA: Mason Crest Publishers, 2009.

Morris, Ting. *Arts and Crafts of the Native Americans*. North Mankato, MN: Smart Apple Media, 2007.

Schomp, Virginia. *The Native Americans*. New York, NY: Marshall Cavendish Benchmark, 2008.

WEB SITES

Kid Info: Native Americans
www.kidinfo.com/american_history/native_americans.html
Follow links to the histories, stories, and customs of many Native American tribes.

Native Americans
edtech.kennesaw.edu/web/natam.html
Find much more information on Native Americans all over the United States.

Index